Programming Principles With C

Master the language of coding with this comprehensive guide to Programming Principles in C

- By Dayanand Gawade

2023

FIRST EDITION

Certificate

"Programming Principles with C" is a comprehensive guide to learning programming written by Dayanand Gawade. This book is perfect for anyone looking to learn programming from scratch or improve their existing programming skills. With over 15 years of teaching experience, Gawade has created an excellent resource that is easy to understand and follow.

This book covers all the fundamental concepts of programming using the C language. The author has used a practical approach, providing clear explanations, practical examples, and hands-on exercises that help readers understand the concepts easily. The book starts with an introduction to programming and the C language, followed by topics such as data types, operators, control structures, arrays, functions, pointers, and file handling.

The book is designed to help beginners get started with programming and gradually build their skills. It is also a great resource for professionals who want to improve their programming skills. The author has included several real-world examples and case studies that demonstrate how programming can be applied in different industries.

Overall, "Programming Principles with C" is an excellent resource for anyone interested in learning programming. It is a must-read for beginners and professionals alike who want to master the fundamentals of programming using the C language.

-Dayanand Gawade

Book Edition: 1 (05-Nov-2023)

Note: This book, "Programming Principles with C," has been recommended by a Professor of Vidyalankar School of Information Technology, Wadala, Mumbai. The college is affiliated with the University of Mumbai and the professor has over 15 years of teaching experience. This book is an excellent resource for beginners and professionals who want to learn programming or improve their programming skills. With its clear explanations, practical examples, and hands-on exercises, it is a must-read for anyone interested in programming.

Index

Note : Next Topics Of C programming Are published on next Edition.

Drop Mail To dayanandgawade@dayanandpvtltd.eu.org For Next Edition Of this Book.

Chapter 1 : Introduction And Fundamentals of C

Topics:

Introduction:
Types of Programming languages, History, features and application. Simple program logic, program development cycle, pseudocode statements and flowchart symbols, sentinel value to end a
program, programming and user environments, evolution of programming models., desirable program characteristics.

Fundamentals:
Structure of a program. Compilation and Execution of a Program, Character Set, identifiers and keywords, data types, constants, variables and arrays, declarations, expressions, statements, Variable definition,
symbolic constants.

Programming Language Levels:

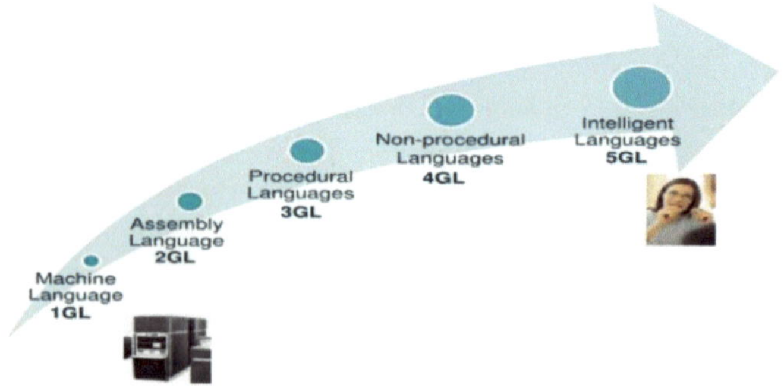

Programming Language Levels – Over View:

Low Level	• Machine specific • Fast execution • Difficult programming and debugging • Long code	Machine Language (1GL)
		Assembly Language (2GL)
High Level	• Human language like • Slower execution • Easier programming and debugging • Shorter code	Procedural languages (3GL)
		Non-procedural languages (4GL)
		Intelligent languages (5GL)

Types of Programming Languages:

1) **Machine Language:**

- Only language Understand by Computers
- Does Not Resemble Human Language
- Difficult to read and write
- Sequence of Bits

2) **Assembly Language**

- Hardware specific
- Mnemonic symbols
- Represent machine code instructions
- Example: Add two numbers
- ADD R1, R2, R3
- Requires translator
- Assembler
3) Maps mnemonics to machine
4) **High Level Language:**

- Computer architecture/hardware
- independent
- Portable
- Easy to read, write, maintain
- Require translator
- Compiler
- Maps statements to machine

History of C :

C was originally developed in the **1970s** by Dennis Ritchie at Bell Telephone Laboratories, Inc. (now a part of AT&T). It is an outgrowth of two earlier languages, called BCPL and B, which were also developed at Bell Laboratories.
Early commercial implementations of C differed somewhat from Kernighan and Ritchie's original definition, resulting in minor incompatibilities between different implementations of the language. These differences diminished the portability that the language attempted to provide. Consequently, the American National Standards Institute (ANSI committee X3J11) has developed a standardized definition of the C language.
In the early 1980s, another high-level programming language, called C++, was developed by Bjarne Stroustrup at the Bell Laboratories. C++ is built upon C, and hence all standard C features are available within C++.

Applications of C :

1. C language is used for creating computer applications

2. Used in writing Embedded softwares

3. Firmware for various electronics, industrial and communications products which use micro-controllers.

4. It is also used in developing verification software, test code, simulators etc. for various applications and hardware products.

5. For Creating Compiles of different Languages which can take input from other language and convert it into lower level machine dependent language.

6. C is used to implement different Operating System Operations.

7. UNIX kernel is completely developed in C Language.

Program Development Cycle:

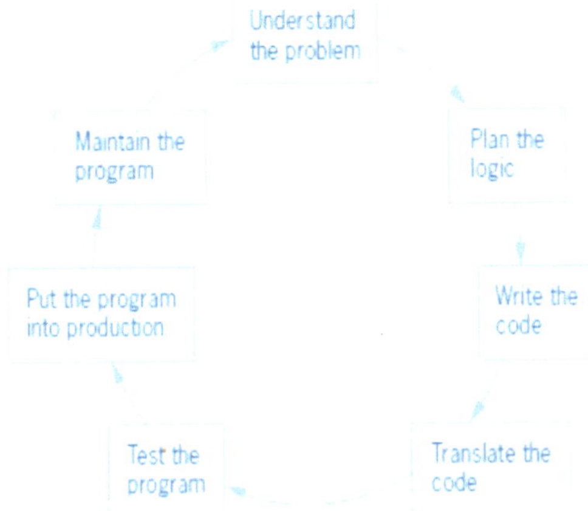

1. ## Understand the problem

Professional computer programmers write programs to satisfy the needs of others, called users or end users. In this phase the developer team must obtain the program requirements from the users and document the requirements.

2. Plan the logic

The heart of the programming process lies in planning the program's logic.During this phase of the process, the programmer plans the steps of the program, deciding what steps to include and how to order them. The two most common planning tools are flowcharts and pseudocode. Planning the logic includes thinking carefully about all the possible data values a program might encounter and how you want the program to handle each scenario.

3. Coding the Program

After the logic is developed, only then can the programmer write the source code for a program. Hundreds of programming languages are available. Programmers choose particular languages because some have built-in capabilities that make them more efficient than others at handling certain types of operations.

4. Translate the code

Even though there are many programming languages, each computer knows only one language—its machine language, which consists of 1s and 0s. So in this phase your program i.e. source code is translated into machine language.

5. Testing the Program

A program that is free of syntax errors is not necessarily free of logical errors. A logical error results when you use a syntactically correct statement but use the wrong one for the current context. In this phase logic of code is tested to see that program is running properly and it produces required outputs with appropriate input data.

6. Put the program into production

Once the program is thoroughly tested and debugged, it is ready for the organization to use. Putting the program into production might mean simply running the program once, if it was written to satisfy a user's request for a special list.
However, the process might take months if the program will be run on a regular basis, or if it is one of a large system of programs being developed.

7. Maintaining the Program

After programs are put into production, making necessary changes is called maintenance. Maintenance can be required for many reasons: for example, because new tax rates are legislated, the format of an input file is altered, or the end user requires additional information not included in the original output specifications.

Chapter 2 : Algorithm and Flowchart

Algorithm and Flowchart :

Algorithm and flowchart are the powerful tools for learning programming. An algorithm is a step-by-step analysis of the process, while a flowchart explains the steps of a program in a graphical way. Algorithm is a step-by-step procedure, which defines a set of instructions to be executed in a certain order to get the desired output. Algorithms are generally created independent of underlying languages, i.e. an algorithm can be implemented in more than one programming language.

Characteristics of an Algorithm :

Not all procedures can be called an algorithm. An algorithm should have the following characteristics −

• Unambiguous − Algorithm should be clear and unambiguous. Each of its steps (or phases), and their inputs/outputs should be clear and must lead to only one meaning.

• Input − An algorithm should have 0 or more well-defined inputs.

• Output − An algorithm should have 1 or more well-defined outputs, and should match the desired output.

• Finiteness − Algorithms must terminate after a finite number of steps.

• Feasibility − Should be feasible with the available resources.

• Independent − An algorithm should have step-by-step directions, which should be independent of any programming code.

Algorithm writing is a process and is executed after the problem domain is well-defined. **Ex 1: Write an algorithm to add 2 numbers and print the sum.**

Step 1 – START.

Step 2 – Read A, B.

Step 3 – SUM=A+B.

Step 4 – Print SUM.

Step 5 – STOP.

Ex 2: Write an algorithm to find the average of 3 numbers.

Step 1 – START.

Step 2 – Read A, B,C.

Step 3 – SUM=A+B+C.

Step 4: AVERAGE=SUM / 3.

Step 5 – Print AVERAGE.

Step 6 – STOP.

Ex 3: write an algorithm to celebrate Teachers Day

Step 1: Start

Step 2: Decide the activities for teachers' day like dance performances, plays, etc.

Step 3: Form groups of students and assign the decided activities from step 2 to each group.

Step 4: Decide the practice timings for each group.

Step 5: Each group to practice as per the timings decided in step 4.

Step 6: Invite the teachers to Teachers' Day celebrations.

Step 7: Perform the activities planned in step 2 on Teachers' Day Step 8: Stop

Flowchart :

The flowchart is a diagram which visually presents the flow of data through processing systems. This means by seeing a flow chart one can know the operations performed and the sequence of these operations in a system.

Flowchart Symbols :

There are 6 basic symbols commonly used in flowcharting of assembly language Programs: Terminal, Process, input/output, Decision, Connector and Predefined Process.

Symbol	Name	Function
	Process	Indicates any type of internal operation inside the Processor or Memory
	input/output	Used for any Input / Output (I/O) operation. Indicates that the computer is to obtain data or output results
	Decision	Used to ask a question that can be answered in a binary format (Yes/No, True/False)
	Connector	Allows the flowchart to be drawn without intersecting lines or without a reverse flow.
	Predefined Process	Used to invoke a subroutine or an Interrupt program.
	Terminal	Indicates the starting or ending of the program, process, or interrupt program
	Flow Lines	Shows direction of flow.

General Rules for Flowcharting :

1. All boxes of the flowchart are connected with Arrows.

2. Flowchart symbols have an entry point on the top of the symbol with no other entry points. The exit point for all flowchart symbols is on the bottom except for the Decision symbol.

3. The Decision symbol has two exit points; these can be on the sides or the bottom and one side.

4. Generally a flowchart will flow from top to bottom. However, an upward flow can be shown as long as it does not exceed 3 symbols.

5. Connectors are used to connect breaks in the flowchart. Examples are:

• From one page to another page.

• From the bottom of the page to the top of the same page.

6. Subroutines and Interrupt programs have their own and independent flowcharts.

7. All flow charts start with a Terminal or Predefined Process (for interrupt programs or subroutines) symbol.

8. All flowcharts end with a terminal or a contentious loop.

Ex1: Flowchart to add sum of two numbers.

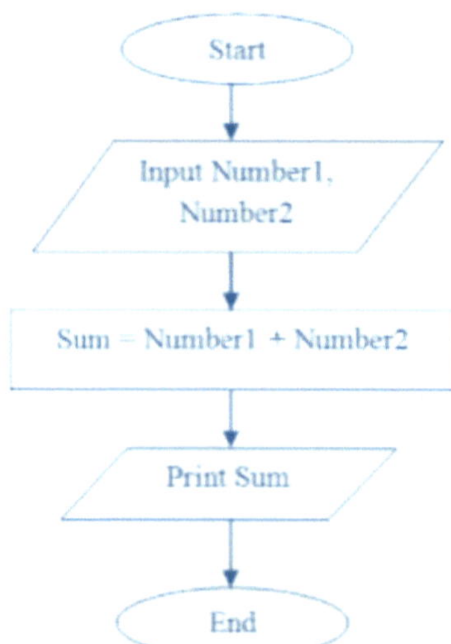

Chapter 3 : Pseudocode

Pseudocode:

Pseudocode is an English-like representation of the logical steps it takes to solve a problem. It is not necessarily follow all the syntax rules of any specific language to write pseudocode.

e.g. a pseudocode representation of a number-doubling problem:

 start

input myNumber

set myAnswer = myNumber * 2 output myAnswer

stop

Pseudocode Standards :

• Programs begin with start and end with stop; these two words are always aligned.

• Whenever a module name is used, it is followed by a set of parentheses.

Modules begin with the module name and end with return. The module name and return are always aligned.

• Each program statement performs one action—for example, input, processing, or output.

• Program statements are indented a few spaces more than start or the module name.

• Each program statement appears on a single line if possible. When this is not possible, continuation lines are indented.

• Program statements begin with lowercase letters.

• No punctuation is used to end statements.

Pseudocode to check whether a given number is even or odd. Start

Print "Enter Any Number to Check, Even or Odd" Read input of a number

If number mod = 0 Print "Number is Even" Else

   Print "Number is Odd"

Sentinel value to end a program :

A program that contains an infinite loop is one that never ends. Such programs can be stopped by giving some predefined values A preselected value that stops the execution of a program is often called a dummy value or a sentinel value.
Many programming languages use the term fe (for file end) to refer to a marker that automatically acts as a sentinel.

For eg:

The program can be used to add up a list of numbers. But the user first has to count up how many numbers are to be added up. This could be annoying. Instead of counting numbers user can specify sentinel value like zero to stop the program. i.e. The user will enter numbers, one by one, and the program will add each number to SUM. The user tells the program to stop by entering a zero. The zero is how the user "signals" that the program should stop looping.

Evolution of programming models :

Two major models or paradigms are used by programmers to develop programs and their procedures:

Procedural programming focuses on the procedures that programmers create. That is, procedural programmers focus on the actions that are carried out—for example, getting input data for an employee and writing the calculations needed to produce a paycheck from the data. Procedural programmers would approach the job of producing a paycheck by breaking down the process into manageable subtasks.

Object-oriented programming focuses on objects, or "things," and describes their features (also called attributes) and behaviors. For example, object-oriented programmers might design a payroll application by thinking about employees and paychecks, and by describing their attributes. Employees have names and Social Security numbers, and paychecks have names and check amounts. Then the programmers would think about the behaviors of employees and paychecks, such as employees getting raises and adding dependents and paychecks being calculated and output. Object-oriented programmers would then build applications from these entities.

DESIRABLE PROGRAM CHARACTERISTICS :

1. Integrity: This refers to the accuracy of the calculations. It should be clear that all other program enhancements will be meaningless if the calculations are not carried out correctly. Thus, the integrity of the calculations is an absolute necessity in any computer program.

2. Clarity: refers to the overall readability of the program, with particular emphasis on its underlying logic. If a program is clearly written, it should be possible for another programmer to follow the program logic without undue effort. It should also be possible for the original author to follow his or her own program after being away from the program for an extended period of time.

3. Simplicity: The clarity and accuracy of a program are usually enhanced by keeping things as simple as possible, consistent with the overall program objectives.

4. Eficiency: is concerned with execution speed and efficient memory utilization.

5. Modularity: Many programs can be broken down into a series of identifiable subtasks. It is good programming practice to implement each of these subtasks as a separate program module. In C, such modules are written as functions.

6. Generality: Usually we will want a program to be as general as possible, within reasonable limits. For example, we may design a program to read in the values of certain key parameters rather than placing fixed values into the program.

Fundamentals Structure of a program :
A C program basically consists of the following parts −

Eg:

Preprocessor Commands Functions

Variables

Statements & Expressions Comments

```c
#include <stdio.h> int main()

{

/* my first program in C */ printf("Hello, World! \n");

return 0;

}
```

The first line of the program #include <stdio.h> is a preprocessor command, which tells a C compiler to include stdio.h file before going to actual compilation.

The next line int main() is the main function where the program execution begins.

The next line /*...*/ will be ignored by the compiler and it has been put to add additional comments in the program. So such lines are called comments in the program.

The next line printf(...) is another function available in C which causes the message "Hello, World!" to be displayed on the screen.

The next line return 0; terminates the main() function and returns the value 0.

Character Set :

C uses the uppercase letters A to Z, the lowercase letters a to z, the digits 0 to 9, and certain special characters as building blocks to form basic program elements (e.g., constants, variables, operators, expressions, etc.). The special characters are listed below.

```
+       -       *       /       =       %       &       #
!       ?       ^       "       '       ~       \       |
<       >       (       )       [       ]       {       }
:       ;       .       ,       _       (blank space)
```

IDENTIFIERS AND KEYWORDS :

- Identifiers are names that are given to various program elements, such as variables, functions and arrays.
- Identifiers consist of letters and digits, in any order, except that the first character must be a letter.
- Both upper- and lowercase letters are permitted.
- Upper- and lowercase letters are not interchangeable (i.e., an uppercase letter is not
- equivalent to the corresponding lowercase letter.)
- The underscore character (-) can also be included, and is considered to be a letter. An underscore is often used in the middle of an identifier.
- An identifier may also begin with an underscore.

Example1:

The following names are valid identifiers:

```
x                 y12              sum_1              _temperature
names             area             tax_rate           TABLE
```

Example2:

The following names are not valid identifiers for the reasons stated.

```
4th                     The first character must be a letter.
'x'                     Illegal characters (').
order-no                Illegal character (-).
error flag              Illegal character (blank space).
```

Chapter 4 : Keywords & DATA TYPES

Keywords:

There are certain reserved words, called keywords, that have standard, predefined meanings in C. These keywords can be used only for their intended purpose; they cannot be used as programmer-defined identifiers.

The standard keywords are

auto	extern	sizeof
break	floatn	static
case	for	struct
char	goto	switch
const	if	typedef
continue	int	union
default	long	unsigned
do	register	void
double	return	volatile
else	short	while
enum	signed	

DATA TYPES :

Data types in c refer to an extensive system used for declaring variables or functions of different types. The type of a variable determines how much space it occupies in storage and how the bit pattern stored is interpreted.

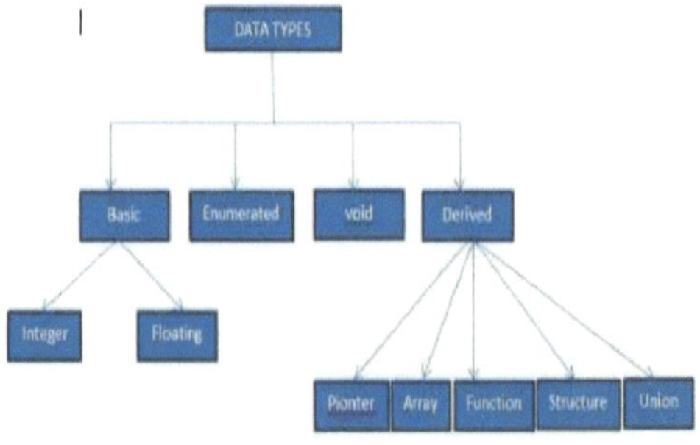

Type	Description
Basic Types	They are arithmetic types and are further classified into: (a) integer types and (b) floating-point types
Enumerated types	They are again arithmetic types and they are used to define variables that can only assign certain discrete integer values throughout the program.
The type void	The type specifier void indicates that no value is available.
Derived types	They include (a) Pointer types, (b) Array types, (c) Structure types, (d) Union types and (e) Function types.

Integer Types

Type	Storage Space	Value Range
Char	1 byte	-128 to 127 or 0 to 255
unsigned char	1 byte	0 to 255
signed char	1 byte	-128 to 127
Int	2 or 4 bytes	-32,768 to 32,767 or -2,147,483,648 to 2,147,483,647
unsigned int	2 or 4 bytes	0 to 65,535 or 0 to 4,294,967,295
Short	2 bytes	-32,768 to 32,767
unsigned short	2 bytes	0 to 65,535
Long	4 bytes	-2,147,483,648 to 2,147,483,647
unsigned long	4 bytes	0 to 4,294,967,295

Floating-Point Types

Type	Storage Space	Value Range	Precision
Float	4 bytes	1.2E-38 to 3.4E+38	6 decimal places
Long	8 bytes	2.3E-308 to 1.7E+308	15 decimal places
Double	10 bytes	3.4E-4932 to 1.1E+4932	19 decimal places

Chapter 5 : Constants

CONSTANTS :

There are four basic types of constants in C. integer constants
floating-point constants character constants string constants
The following rules apply to all numeric-type constants.
Commas and blank spaces cannot be included within the constant.
The constant can be preceded by a minus (-) sign if desired. (Actually the minus sign is an operator
that changes the sign of a positive constant, though it can be thought of as a part of the constant
itself.)
The value of a constant cannot exceed specified minimum and maximum bounds. For each type of
constant, these bounds will vary from one C compiler to another.

1. Integer Constants

An integer constant is an integer-valued number. Thus it consists of a sequence of
digits. Integer constants can be written in three different number systems: decimal (base 10), octal
(base 8) and hexadecimal (base 16). Some valid decimal integer constants:
0 12 -234 76543 -8901
The following decimal integer constants are written incorrectly for the reasons stated.

12,245	illegal character (,).
36.0	illegal character (.).
10 20 30	illegal character (blank space).
123-45-6789	illegal character (-).
0900	the first digit cannot be a zero.

Unsigned and Long Integer Constants :

Unsigned integer constants may exceed the magnitude of ordinary integer constants by
approximately a factor of 2, though they may not be negative.* An unsigned integer constant can be
identified by appending the letter U (either upper- or lowercase) to the end of the constant.
Long integer constants may exceed the magnitude of ordinary integer constants, but require more
memory within the computer. To create a long integer constant by appending the letter L (either
upper- or lowercase) to the end of the constant.
Some unsigned and long integer constants are shown below
500000U (decimal unsigned)
　　123456789L (Decimal Long)

　　123456789UL (Decimal unsigned long)

2. Floating-Point Constants :

A floating-point constant is a base- 10 number that contains either a decimal point or an exponent (or
both).
Some valid floating-point constants are shown below.

0.	1.	0.2	827.602
50000.	0.000743	12.3	315.0066
2E-8	0.006e-3	1.6667E+8	.12121212e12

The following are not valid floating-point constants for the reasons stated.

1	Either a decimal point or an exponent must be present
1,000.0	Illegal character (,)
2E+10.2	The exponent must be an integer quantity (it cannot contain a decimal point)
3E 10	Illegal character (blank space) in the exponent.

3. Character Constants

A **character constant** is a single character, enclosed in apostrophes (i.e., single quotation marks). Some character constants are shown below:

'A'   'x'   '3'   '?'   ' '

Character constants have integer values that are determined by the computer's particular character set. Most computers make use of the ASCII (i.e., American Standard Code for Information Interchange) character set, in which each individual character is numerically encoded with its own unique 7-bit combination (hence a total of $2^7 = 128$ different characters).

Some character constants and their corresponding values, as defined by the ASCII character set, are shown below.

Constant	Value
'A'	65
'x'	120
'3'	51
'?'	63
' '	32

Escape Sequences :

An escape sequence always begins with a backward slash(\) and is followed by one or more special characters.

Character	Escape Sequence	ASCII Value
bell (alert)	\a	007
backspace	\b	008
horizontal tab	\t	009
vertical tab	\v	011
newline (line feed)	\n	010
form feed	\f	012
carriage return	\r	013
quotation mark (")	\"	034
apostrophe (')	\'	039
question mark (?)	\?	063
backslash (\)	\\	092
null	\0	000

String Constants :

A ***string constant*** consists of any number of consecutive characters (including none), enclosed in (double) quotation marks. Some string constants are shown below.

```
"green"        "Washington, D.C. 20005"      "270-32-3456"
"$19.95"       "THE CORRECT ANSWER IS:"       "2*(I+3)/J"
"     "        "Line 1\nLine 2\nLine 3"       ""
```

the string constant "Line 1\nLine 2\nLine 3" extends over three lines, because of the newline characters that are embedded within the string. Thus, this string would be displayed as

Line 1
Line 2
Line 3

Chapter 6: VARIABLES AND ARRAYS

VARIABLES AND ARRAYS :

A variable is an identifier that is used to represent a single data item; i.e., a numerical quantity or a character constant within a designated portion of the program.
The data item must be assigned to the variable at some point in the program.
The data item can then be accessed later in the program simply by referring to the variable name.
A given variable can be assigned different data items at various places within the program.
Thus, the information represented by the variable can change during the execution of the program.
However, the data type associated with the variable cannot change.
Example:
A C program contains the following lines

```
int a, b, c;
char d;

. . .

a = 3;
b = 5;
c = a + b;
d = 'a';

. . .

a = 4;
b = 2;
c = a - b;
d = 'W';
```

The first two lines are type declarations, which state that a, b and c are integer variables, and that d is a char-type variable.

The next four lines cause the following things to happen: the integer quantity 3 is assigned to a, 5 is assigned to b, and the quantity represented by the sum a + b (i.e., 8) is assigned to c. The character 'a' is then assigned to d.

The last four lines redefine the values assigned to the variables as follows: the integer quantity 4 is assigned to a, replacing the earlier value, 3; then 2 is assigned to b, replacing the earlier value, 5; then the difference between a and b (i.e., 2) is assigned to c, replacing the earlier value, 8. Finally, the character ' W' is assigned to d, replacing the earlier character, ' a '

.

Array

An array is an identifier that refers to a *collection* of data items that all have the same name. The data items must all be of the same type (e.g., all integers, all characters, etc.).

The individual data items are represented by their corresponding *array-elements* (i.e., the first data item is represented by the first array element, etc.).

The individual array elements are distinguished from one another by the value that is assigned to a **subscript.**

Declaration :

A declaration associates a group of variables with a specific data type. All variables must be declared before they can appear in executable statements.

A declaration consists of a data type, followed by one or more variable names, ending with a semicolon.

Each array variable must be followed by a pair of square brackets, containing a positive integer which specifies the size (i.e., the number of elements) of the array.

A C program contains the following type declarations

int a, b, c ;
float root 1 , root2;
char flag , text [80] ;

These declarations could also have been written as follows.

```
              int a;
              int b;
           float rootl;
            float rootl;

          float root2;
           char flag;
           char text[80];
```

Chapter 7: EXPRESSIONS &STATEMENTS

EXPRESSIONS :

An *expression* represents a single data item, such as a number or a character. The expression may consist of a single entity, such as a constant, a variable, an array element or a reference to a function. It may also consist of some combination of such entities, interconnected by one or more *operators.* Expressions can also represent logical conditions that are either true or false.
However, in C the conditions true and false are represented by the integer values 1 and 0, respectively.

Some simple expressions are shown below.
a + b x
= y
c = a + b x <= y
x == Y
i=i+1

STATEMENTS:

A statement causes the computer to carry out some action. There are three different classes of statements in C. They are expression statements, compound statements and control statements. An expression statement consists of an expression followed by a semicolon.

Some expression statements are shown below.
a = 3;
c = a + b ; i++;
A **compound statement** consists of several individual statements enclosed within a pair of braces { }. The compound statement provides a capability for embedding statements within other statements. Unlike an expression statement, a compound statement does not end with a semicolon. A typical compound statement is shown below.
{
p i = 3.141593;
circumference = 2. * p i * radius; area = p i * radius * radius;
}

Control statements are used to create special program features, such **as** logical tests, loops and branches
. if(a>b)
{
else
{
printf("first no is greater");
}
printf("secod no is greater");
}

SYMBOLIC CONSTANTS:

A symbolic constant is a name that substitutes for a sequence of characters. The characters may represent a numeric constant, a character constant or a string constant. Thus, a symbolic constant allows a name to appear in place of a numeric constant, a character constant or a string. When a program is
compiled, each occurrence of a symbolic constant is replaced by its corresponding character sequence. Symbolic constants are usually defined at the beginning of a program.
A symbolic constant is defined by writing
#define name text
where name represents a symbolic name, typically written in uppercase letters, and text represents the sequence of characters that is associated with the symbolic name.
A C program contains the following symbolic constant definitions.
#define TAXRATE 0.23 #define P I 3.141593 #define TRUE 1
#define FALSE 0
#define FRIEND "Susan"
Now suppose that the program contains the statement
area = PI * radius * radius;
During the compilation process, each occurrence of a symbolic constant will be replaced by its corresponding text. Thus, the above statement will become
area = 3.141593 * radius * radius;

Typedef :

typedef is used to define new data type names to make a program more readable to the programmer.
```
#include<stdio.h>
int main()
{
int money;
money=2;
}
```

```
#include<stdio.h>
int main()
{
typedef int Pounds;
Pounds money=2;
}
```
These examples are treated as same by the compiler.

Typecasting :

Converting one data type into another is known as type casting or, type-conversion. For example, if you want to store a 'long' value into a simple integer then you can type cast 'long' to 'int'. You can convert the values from one type to another explicitly using the cast operator as follows −

Syntax : (type_name) expression;
Consider the following example where the cast operator causes the division of one integer variable by another to be performed as a floating-point operation –

```
#include <stdio.h>
main() {
int sum = 17, count = 5;
double mean;
mean = (double) sum / count;
printf("Value of mean : %f\n", mean );
}
```

Output: Value of mean : 3.400000
It should be noted here that the cast operator has precedence over division, so the value of sum is first converted to type double and finally it gets divided by count yielding a double value.

Question Bank

1. What are different types of programming language? Explain in detail.

2. Explain any five features of C language.

3. What are the applications of C language?

4. What are the different phases of program development cycle? Explain in detail.

5. What do you mean by sentinel value? Explain in detail.

6. What are different desirable program characteristics?

7. Explain basic structure of a C program.

8. What are identifiers? What are naming rules for identifiers?

9. Explain different basic data types in C.

10. Explain different types of constants in C.

11. What are escape sequences? Explain.

12. What are variables? Explain with example.

13. What are different types of statements in C?

14. What are symbolic constants? Explain with example.

15. Explain different symbols in flowchart?

16. Draw a flowchart and a pseudo code of a program that doubles the number.

17. What is a statement in C? Explain Different classes of statements in C.

18. What do you understand from simple program logic? Discuss with suitable example.

19. What are the rules for writing identifiers?

20. What are constants in c? Discuss various types of constants used in c.

21. Write a pseudo code to find out the factorial of a number.

22. What do you understand from simple program logic? Discuss with suitable example.

23. How is the variable declared and used in an expression?

24. What is a statements in C? Explain Different classes of statements in C.

25. Determine if the following identifiers are valid in C
a) Record1
b) $tax

c) 123-45-6789
d) Address and name
e) File_3

26. Determine if the following constants are valid in C
a) 27,822
b) 0.8E 8
c) "Name:
d) "1.3e-12"
e) 0xBCFDAL
27. What is typecasting?
28. Explain the structure of C programming with an example.
29. Draw a flowchart to find the circumference of a circle.
30. Differentiate between a Pseudocode and a flowchart.

Multiple Choice Questions

1. **Who is father of C Language?**

   a. Bjarne Stroustrup

   b. James A. Gosling
   c. Dennis Ritchie
   d. Dr. E.F. Codd

   2. Which of the following is not a valid variable name declaration?
   a. int a3;

   b. int 3a;

   c. int A3;

d. None of the mentioned

3. Variable names beginning with underscore is not encouraged. Why?
a. It is not standardized

b. To avoid conflicts since assemblers and loaders use such names

c. To avoid conflicts since library routines use such names
d. To avoid conflicts with environment variables of an operating system

4. All keywords in C are in
a. LowerCase letters

b. UpperCase letters

c. CamelCase letters